Discipling Through Your Disability

by Anita Allen-Penn, Ph. D.

©2016, Anita Allen-Penn, Ph. D.
All Rights Reserved

ISBN: 978-1-936497-31-7

Searchlight Press
Who are you looking for?
Publishers of thoughtful Christian books since 1994.
PO Box 554
Henderson, TX 75652-0554
214.662.5494
www.Searchlight-Press.com
www.JohnCunyus.com

**Dr. Anita Allen-Penn
and family**

Dedication

This book is dedicated to the mothers, fathers, grandparents, and families all over the world who share this journey of nurturing their child through their medical struggles and set-backs into becoming all that God has designed them to be.

Table of Contents

Preface	5
Part One A Mother's Diary	9
Part Two I Am Determined!	21
Part Three Matters of the Heart	31
Part Four A Better Understanding	57
Part Five Christian Parenting	81
Steal Away to Some Secret Place (A poem by Fredna Hadley Allen)	109
About Dr Anita Allen-Penn	110
With Special Thanks	112

Preface

As parents we have plans, aspirations, and beliefs that our children will do great things, become important people, be trend-setters and world changers. We look forward to them following in our footsteps through mannerisms, sporting activities, and lifestyle choices. We imagine they will have physical traits that we recognize as our own or as another immediate family member.

> How do you balance love and fear when faced with the fact that your child has a genetic disorder that will affect their entire life?

But what happens to those desires when faced with the reality that your child has a chronic illness? How do you balance love and fear when faced with the fact that your child has a genetic disorder that will affect their entire life? How do you handle the emotional strain of making life-saving decisions without having time to embrace the information that is being thrown at you? All while wondering, why me?

The answer is simply to trust that God knows what you need, and when you need it. Trusting God is easy to say, but sometimes hard to do, especially, when you can't understand why God has placed you in this situation.

In my case, I was advised that my son would be born with a Congenital Heart Defect (CHD). And this particular Heart Defect is commonly found in people with Down syndrome. This diagnosis somewhat prepared me for the CHD and Down syndrome, but I was absolutely unprepared for the journey that would come along with it.

When reality sets in that there is something wrong with my child, it does not matter what the doctors have already told you, and how prepared you think you are…your mental and emotional capacities are no longer the same.

Being a divorced mother of three, and a ministry-minded Christian woman is very challenging. Everyone has their demands and expectations of who they need you to be for them. It is a challenge recognizing that God has chosen me to raise and nurture three children, and serve in a specific teaching and preaching ministry, while not allowing circumstances of life to hinder HIS plan for me.

It can become a struggle to balance everyone else's needs and your own burning desire to do the work that

GOD has called you to do – a work that formed, grew, and became alive in my belly…just as this fragile, precious, child did. Little did I know an innocent six pound baby boy, who was as imperfect as medical science could predict, would be the magnificently perfect example and teacher that God would use to prepare me for His work. Nicholas is here to teach us how to Disciple Through Your Disability.

NOTES

Part One—A Mother's Diary

"I knew before I formed you in your mother?s womb. Before you were born I set you apart and appointed you as my prophet to the nations."
　　　　　　　Jeremiah 1:5 (NLT)

Around the twenty-second week of my second pregnancy I was told by a neonatologist that my "Baby B" had a sagging belly and his heart was not developing properly. He said I needed to see a pediatric cardiologist who would take a closer look at Baby B's heart and give me a more accurate diagnosis. As he left the examination room to give me time to dress, I stood there stunned and scared. When he returned, he let me know that he had made my appointment for that same afternoon. He handed me a copy of directions from Mapquest, and wished me luck. As I exited the office, the faces of the staff were solemn and carried the look of what I was thinking, "My baby is not going to live." I left there alone and confused and not knowing that my life was about to change forever.

While heading to the pediatric cardiologists office I called my god-mother to let her know I would be late picking up my 2 year old. I explained the situation without any emotion. I don't remember much of that conversation but obviously I told her where I was headed. As I arrived to the office, much to my amazement she was there. She had brought her daughter to be with me as I got a more complete diagnosis…and she has been by my side every since.

Baby B had already claimed the hearts of two people.

I was given another sonogram and fetal ultra sound with a primary focus on Baby B's heart. It seemed like it took three hours, though it was probably closer to 30 minutes. I was so scared from anticipating the morbid news I anticipated receiving. I just wanted the doctor to hurry up and tell me that my baby was going to die and let me go home. However, she didn't. She did confirm that he had a heart defect that was common and repairable—as if it were no big deal. I remember thinking "how in the world can she be so calm? Surely she's crazy."

> **My mind began to drift and I began to think of a million questions, but I could not verbalize even one. I felt like I was having an out-of-body experience.**

My mind began to drift and I began to think of a million questions, but I could not verbalize even one. I felt like I was having an out-of-body experience. It seemed as though I was watching my god-sister talk to the doctor and every now and then I would hear a word or a phrase. I couldn't focus. All I could think of is "Why me, why my baby?" But the one phrase I did catch quite clearly was "Down syndrome."

Leaving that office visit I knew that there was a

definite Congenital Heart Defect (CHD), and a possible genetic disability. What kind of blow was the Lord dealing me? I know I hadn't been the best Christian, but surely I wasn't one of the worst! I'd always been told not to question God, but today I had to break that rule. I wanted to know, "why me?" Some time passed before I heard my answer from God, when in my quiet place, He clearly said, "Why not you?"

One of the most natural desires for a woman is to marry the perfect man, live in a beautiful home, and raise perfect well mannered successful children. Many have made it, but not me. This was a pivotal moment in this chapter of my life. When I consider God's answer of "why not you," I just chuckle. My family and the village of extended family consist of several educators, active and retired. Baby B would be born into a family that offers him a personal team of teachers and therapists. Had God actually been preparing our family for such a time as this, to love, teach, and nurture Baby B?

"But Jesus overheard them and said to Jairus, "Don't be afraid. Just have faith."
                    Mark 5:38 (NLT)

Finding out that one of the babies I was carrying in

my womb was not developing properly was overwhelming. I had a wonderful, Christian OBGYN who would pray for me and with me when I needed it.

> ...he asked me "Would you abort your baby if you knew he had Down syndrome?"
>
> I immediately said "No!"

I remember my last visit with him when he told me it would be best for me to find a doctor who practiced in the hospital where Baby B needed to be delivered due to his CHD. My doctor explained that now, I needed to start making decisions based on what would be best for my baby and his unexpected conditions.

I remember telling him that a genetic specialist had talked to me about having a procedure done called an amniocentesis in order to find out if the baby had Down syndrome. So far it was just a possibility, due to the type of heart defect he had been diagnosed with. I fought back tears as I explained my options. In turn he asked me "Would you abort your baby if you knew he had Down syndrome?"

I immediately said "No!"

With his cool and calm demeanor he asked, "Then why do you need to know before he's born, and risk the health of Baby A?"

From that point forward, I began to look at what I called fear as just an uncertainty. As I reflect, I must admit that God is awesome. Because out of all the fears I had for one baby, I did not have those same fears for the other baby, who was growing in my womb at the same time. How does a body produce one healthy child and one child with abnormalities at the same time? Who else can orchestrate such a thing other than God? Both children, given the same everything at the same time…and be extremely different. Different gender, different health, and even a different skin tone! Only God can do something as intricate as that. I had to learn to turn my fears and uncertainties over to Him.

Much to my surprise, God in His infinite wisdom began to disciple me for ministry. He used an imperfect baby boy to draw me closer to a perfect God. I had to settle it in my heart that God was all I needed, because in this situation, God was all I had. It didn't matter how much love, how many hugs and kisses, or how many tears I would shed. I couldn't fix my baby. No matter how much I loved him, I couldn't take his illnesses away from him. I couldn't pinch myself and wake up from a bad dream, and I couldn't run to my parents to fix it. All I had was God. I had to rely on what I had been taught over the years—that Jesus is sitting at the right hand of God, interceding on my behalf. I needed to completely depend on God alone.

"By faith we understand that the entire universe was formed at God's command, that what we now see did not come from anything that can be seen."
Hebrews 11:3 (NLT)

I tried to understand all of the information that began to come my way –solicited and unsolicited. I needed God to know that I took raising one of His 'Special Babies" seriously and would consult Him on all decisions that had to be made. But sometimes decisions had to be made very quickly, so I prayed that the Holy Spirit would fill me so I had immediate understanding and discernment.

The day Babies A & B were born I remember each one of them having their own team of nurses. I had already given my parents directions to go with each one of my babies. I wasn't concerned about myself because I knew that God had a job for me to do. I later felt sorry for the staff, because my parents probably watched them like hawks and questioned every move.

About 7 hours after birth, I was able to visit Baby B—my sweet Nicholas. When I found out that I couldn't hold him, it broke my heart. All I could do was watch him sleep as monitors lit up and sung out. I didn't know what to do other than believe God had things under control. I was able to keep his twin sister Nia in the hospital room with me, but as I held her all I could think about was how I couldn't hold Nicholas.

> **That phone call made things for real. Nicholas is here, he's been tested, and he's broken.**

All the staff was advising me to get as much rest as possible because I had a long road ahead of me. And Nicholas was experiencing more difficulties than expected. He had to have several tests in order for the doctors to give his full diagnosis.

Bright and early the very next morning after his birth, at exactly 7:30am, my hospital room phone rang. It was the on-duty doctor for the weekly am shift. She verified who I was, who she was, and proceeded to advise me that Nicholas indeed had a Complete Atrioventricular Heart Defect, Down syndrome (Trisomy 21), and Hirschsprung's disease. All I could say was, "O.K."

An immediate wave of emotions began to stir up inside of me.. That phone call made things for real. Nicholas is here, he's been tested, and he's broken. I remember thinking that I was prepared for the CHD, kind of prepared for Down syndrome, but what in the heck is Hirshsprung's disease? And where did it come from? I was overwhelmed with emotions that I could not harness, nor explain.

After hanging up the phone I told my parents and my nurse that I wanted to take a shower before going to visit Nicholas in the NICU. My hospital bathroom would become my temporary prayer closet. I was just swelling up inside with heartache and confusion. My baby boy had so many challenges ahead of him. His body would have to endure things that I couldn't imagine. I just needed to cry. I needed to pray. I needed to call out to my Savior. I needed God's help and I needed it in a major manner. And with urgency! I had to pray. I couldn't trust anybody else's prayers…I needed to have a talk with Jesus.

I assured my mother and the nurse that I could shower without any assistance. After locking the bathroom door my tears immediately started to flood my eyes. I turned on the water in the sink and in the shower as strong as it would flow. I was trying to drown out the wailing cry that was forming in the pit of my empty belly. In that moment I cried out to the Lord like I never had before. I verbally reaffirmed that I knew His power and that I needed Him to heal my baby! I needed Him to fix my baby's broken heart and to heal his little body from whatever else that was going on inside of him. I made a promised God that I didn't take it lightly that He has given me an assignment of mothering a child that needed extra attention. I recognized that God was drawing me closer to Him.

As I prayed, my tears cleansed my mind, and I stood in the shower boldly reconfirming my faith in the Word of God. I called out my son's name; "Nicholas," whose name means "Warrior" Nicholas was here to fight for his life and to use his disabilities to Disciple his mother.

In order to understand why I refer to Nicholas as a Disciple, we need to understand the meaning of the word disciple. I once read an article written by Dr. Richard J. Krejeir that described a disciple as "one who grows in Christ and in so doing models and teaches Christians the precepts of the Bible, prayer, doctrine, relationships, Christian living, service, and worship, to name the main ones."

Just in the first few days of his life, Nicholas had begun to teach me to pray in a mighty way. I couldn't hold him for nearly the first week of his life and while just sitting with him and watching him sleep, I began to pray more, read God's Word more, and consider this new chapter in my life. The main purpose of Christian Discipleship is that the person who is being disciple ends up being more like Christ.

> When I think of the lessons Nicholas teaches me, he is definitely a disciple. Everyday he makes me reflect on what's really important.

When I think of the lessons Nicholas teaches me, he is definitely a disciple. Everyday he makes me reflect on what's really important. Christ gave us a perfect example of how to handle suffering, trials, and pain. Ironically, my little "disciple" teaches me daily how to handle suffering, trials, and pain. Nicholas is teaching me how to emulate the character of Christ.

"To this you were called, because Christ suffered for you, leaving you an example that you should follow in His steps."
                    1Peter 2:21 (NLT)

The word disciple comes from the Latin word *discipulus*, meaning someone who pledges to be a learner. In my case I am the one being discipled: a mother, following the teaching of her son, with a commitment to learn what God has for me to learn.

When Nicholas was first born, his body couldn't keep a healthy temperature on its own. Seeing him for the first time, he was lying in a bed on his belly, with a heat lamp overhead that was designed to keep him warm. It reminded me of a toaster oven. I remember thinking that without this light over Nicholas, he would not rest peacefully. Then I reflected on the fact that without the light of Jesus overhead warming me with His love, I could not have had any peace during those first several months. From the first time I met my son in his toaster oven bed, he has been guiding me closer to Christ. Nicholas was beginning his journey to Disciple Through His Disability.

Part Two—I Am Determined

"We are pressed on every side by troubles, but we are not crushed. We are perplexed, but not driven to despair. We are hunted down, but never abandoned by God. We get knocked down, but we are not destroyed."
　　　　　　2 Corinthians 4:8-10 (NLT)

Have you ever considered your own defects? We all have at least one. It may not be genetic or recognized by society as a defect. We all have something that holds us back from doing and giving God our all.

Would you identify with being unhealthy, depressed, fearful, brokenhearted, ashamed, doubtful, or unconfident? Even in our defective state we should still be determined to be a disciple for Christ. It may be our defect that draws another. Our defect may make us more credible and understanding of another person's circumstance. Being a Christian disciple requires us to follow Jesus' teachings, to be fruitful, to love others and make disciples. When we put Jesus first in everything, it calls for us to be set apart from the world.

> It may be our defect that draws another. Our defect may make us more credible and understanding of another person's circumstance.

My son doesn't view the world through the window of traditional society. He is just a little boy who is trying to do everything his twin sister is doing. He doesn't realize that he isn't on her level or that he isn't typical---and she doesn't treat him like he isn't. I thank God for giving him a twin sister. She has been his best therapist and pint-sized advocate.

The world has expectations of children at different ages and stages of his life; however, he simply can't meet most of them. But when he does have moments of triumph, we are his overjoyed over-the-top cheerleaders. To see him smile because he's proud of himself makes his accomplishments worth the wait. Just like a disciple of Christ needs to be set apart from the world, I have needed to be set apart from the worlds expectations of my son. The world can be a mean cold place sometimes. But I must admit that even in those tough times, Nicholas can smile and melt a hardened heart. Discipleship is also reciprocal. I've seen signs posted around churches that say, "Each one, reach one," and it reminds me that once we are disciple we are supposed to disciple another.

Following Jesus' teaching is simply being obedient to the Word. Jesus was a perfect example because he showed obedience to His Father, even unto death. Children are so innocent and pure until we parents allow our feelings, thoughts, insecurities, and emotions to affect their personalities. However, Nicholas doesn't know how to live without Down syndrome. His differences were designed by God while he was in my womb. I say he has "Designer Genes." He is an original. Nobody can duplicate what he does. Yes, Nicholas has Down syndrome, and some days it has him. Sometimes he cannot process tasks and activities in his mind, and he is defeated.

What I have learned from watching him is that if I claim to be a Christian, I don't get to decide if I am going to have God in my life from day to day. Nicholas cannot choose to put down his diagnosis and he has taught me not to put down my quest for following God. Some days are tougher than others—for Nicholas and for me. I've learned that no matter what we are faced with, we should be obediently grounded in God's Word.

Everyday Nicholas wakes up—he awakes with his disabilities, but it doesn't change who he is or how he acts, or how he responds to others. We can learn a lot from that! As we face suffering and heartache we can trust God to be there. When I see my son suffering from surgeries and doctor visits stemming from his heart defect or various others problems I love the determination he has to succeed. No day is the same. We've learned to live with the unexpected. And we've learned mostly through trial and error. We test different approaches and we adapt to what works for him. Some days are tougher than others for our family, but I just reflect on how God is patient with me. My disabilities cause me to be hard to deal with, uncooperative and challenging also.

> "Yes I am the vine; you are the branches. Those who remain in me, and I in them, will produce much fruit. For apart from me you can do nothing. Anyone who does not remain in me is thrown away like a useless branch and withers. Such branches are gathered into a pile to be burned. But if you remain in me and my words remain in you, you may ask for anything you want and it will be granted! When you produce much fruit, you are my true disciples. This brings great glory to my Father."
> John 15:5-8 (NLT)

> **Watching Nicholas live with his disabilities and still be able to thrive is amazing to me. He doesn't know how to take advantage of God or other people. All he knows is to keep trying and give his best effort possible.**

I love Nicholas' never-give-up attitude. He shows me how to be fruitful. He teaches me that because we are designed by God that whatever disabilities we may have, God still grants us many abilities. Watching Nicholas live with his disabilities and still be able to thrive is amazing to me. He doesn't know how to take advantage of God or other people. All he knows is to keep trying and give his best effort possible.

So many times I have allowed my current circumstances to dictate my attitude, ultimately affecting my Christian witnessing. When I see my son struggling with what seems to be a simple task, my heart just aches. I'm afraid of how long it will take or if he will ever meet that goal. I must admit that when I see him struggling I just want to scoop him up in my arms and cry.

But Nicholas doesn't hold pity parties. He chooses to fight. He chooses fruitfulness. He chooses to work with his disabilities and not to let them work against him. Nicholas is always content. His disabilities don't keep him from pressing forward. They aren't his inner crutch. I strive to give back to him double of what he offers me.

I'm reminded of a time when Nicholas asked me if he could take my paper plate to the trash can. My first instinct was to say "no" because he had a lot of balance issues. I knew that he had seen his sister help me many times before, and he just wanted his chance at helping his Momma. So I said "Yes." As

I handed him the paper plate he took it in both hands

holding it steady and close to his chest. He slowly and carefully walked towards the trash can which may have been about 20 steps away. I held my breath and prayed he would make it without falling or dropping the plate. I just wanted him to have another success. Both of his sisters stopped what they were doing and watched. With each step our excitement was building…our smiles were getting wider…then finally, he made it!

We cheered and laughed and his smile said how proud he was of himself. Proud. Proud that he had done the same things he sees his sisters doing. I looked at him in that moment and wondered what would this world be like if we all had that type of determination to render service to one another? How many opportunities do we miss out on to disciple others to Christ, all because we don't love each other enough?

Nicholas expressed his love by taking an uneasy walk to the trash can. I learned a valuable lesson that day. Love is powerful. God loves Nicholas so much that He allowed him to have a successful moment because he had a heart to serve. He had a driven will to accomplish a goal. For many of us, Nic's goal of throwing away some trash may seem meaningless. However, my little disciple taught me that in spite of my personal disabilities, I can still overcome problems or obstacles. That I must set my goal---and be determined to successfully complete it.

> *"You are the light of the world—like a city on a hilltop that cannot be hidden. No one lights a lamp and then puts it under a basket. Instead, a lamp is placed on a stand, where it gives light to everyone in the house. In the same way, let your good deeds shine out for all to see, so that everyone will praise your Heavenly Father."*
>
> Matthew 5:14-16 (NLT)

> **When I look at him falling behind, God reminds me to consider the rear view mirror of my life with Nic.**

Nicholas is a bright light. And he doesn't make it shine, he lets it shine. Nicholas is an attention grabber. I don't put him on a pedestal, but I don't hide him and his disabilities either. I don't hide the fact that he has several developmental delays. Nor do I hide the fact that his disabilities delay him from accomplishing things at the rate of his peers.

When I look at him falling behind, God reminds me to consider the rear view mirror of my life with Nic. Nicholas let his light shine as he lay on a warming bed for the first 42 days of his life, fighting to live with a failing heart and a broken belly. His light shined as he was poked in every part of his little body—even as the IV's went into his scalp. Nicholas let his light shine when at a week old he went through surgery for a colostomy. He let his light shine as he fearlessly went through open heart surgery at 5 months old and barely weighing 10 pounds.

Ultimately, before two years old, Nicholas had six surgeries for various health issues. By God's grace each time a surgery was completed, the surgeons said, "It went better than we expected." That same statement came from different surgeons and I knew that my God had not left Nicholas' side. It was as if God was telling me, "I've already taken care of this, you're just going through the motions and emotions."

NOTES

Discipling Through Your Disability, 30

Part Three---Matters of the Heart

"Even if we feel guilty, God is greater than our feelings, and He knows everything."
1 John 3:20 (NLT)

As I tried to figure out why I have a child with disabilities, I ask myself, "Why has God done this to me?"

> **I've read that a lot of mothers think they did something wrong during pregnancy, but I felt like this happened due to a lifetime of my poor choices. Such a wave of guilt consumed me.**

What did I do so bad that God had to punish my child with a defective heart and a genetic disorder? Have all my sins, seen and unseen been rolled up into one big sin and I've forced God to give me an imperfect child? I felt guilty. I've read that a lot of mothers think they did something wrong during pregnancy, but I felt like this happened due to a lifetime of my poor choices. Such a wave of guilt consumed me.

Though the genetic professionals could give me scientific evidence that none of Nicholas' conditions were my fault, I still felt like all of my bad deeds had finally caught up with me. I am guilty of failed marriages, inappropriate relationships, and of not considering how my actions and decisions would affect others. I am guilty of not always telling the truth, no matter who my lies may have hurt. I have disappointed those that I love most.

I believed that maybe if I had loved God more and been a more effective witness, this never would have happened. If I had been financially responsible and supported the church regularly this never would have happened. I f I had visited the sick, or stood on the usher board, or fed the needy, etc…this never would have happened. Guilty of not following through on promises. Guilty of not always being honest with my loved ones and friends. Guilty. Guilty. Guilty.

Everything I have been guilty of doing or not doing must have had a direct connection to the type of son the Lord sent me. Imperfect. Defective. Disabled. And now, everyone will know my guilt, my shame, my embarrassment---they will see my truth exposed as soon as they see my son.

Guilt can make you remember things from your past that you had actually forgotten. However, it also brings back memories of times that God has already forgiven you. I understood that I didn't share in the scientific reason for my son's defects, but I felt like I had offered a negative spiritual contribution. It's funny how we can come up with all the reasons why God allows things to happen in our lives to punish us.

However, we find it hard to see how much God loves us when He allows is to go through trials. After finally accepting the fact that God forgets repented past sins, I was able to see the joy in having Nicholas. Everyone doesn't get a baby like this. I was able to see that God was entrusting me with one of his special designs. I began to think of Nicholas as a "Designer's Original." The blood of Jesus has washed away my guilt and shame. I now see that throughout my life, God was actually preparing me for Nicholas.

"Anger is cruel, and wrath is like a flood, but jealousy is even more dangerous"
Proverbs 27:4 (NLT)

It may be hard for some parents to admit that they are anything but proud of their young children. I have family and friends with beautiful, brilliant, witty, intelligent, delightful, disability-free children. The mothers went through normal pregnancies and had perfectly healthy children.

I will admit – sometimes I get jealous. I envy them at times simply because they can sit down at dinner and have an uneventful experience. On the few occasions I have said to them that I wished I had that type of relationship with Nicholas, their response is "Oh, there's nothing wrong with Nic, he'll be okay."

But they just don't know what I go through everyday. I am very proud of Nicholas and the progress he has made, but I can honestly say that this lifestyle is not what I had planned for. Yes, I do get jealous when Nicholas can't seem to fit in with other children because of his physical limitations.

A few months ago my kids were invited to a birthday party at a local bounce house facility. The week before the party, I called the Mom to verify that she had planned for me to bring all 3 of my children. In her true form she chastised me for even asking.

When we arrived to the party one of the first signs I noticed said "socks only." Immediately I started to cringe because Nicholas has had many delays due to poor balance. I was afraid with socks on he wouldn't be able to participate like the typical kids because it would be slippery. As his sisters began to take off their shoes, he followed. I began to direct the girls that they had to hold their brother's hand. And they did—until they got inside. Once they saw all the bounce houses their excitement sent them running full speed ahead, leaving Nicholas behind and alone.

But to my surprise, the floor was carpeted. My heart was still sad, because there was no way Nicholas could jump in a bounce house with other kids jumping. What was I thinking about bringing my baby here! My heart just hurt, as I watched my son just sit in there in the middle of the jump area while the other kids jumped and played all around him.

To me it wasn't fair that he couldn't jump too. It wasn't fair that his only activity was to move out the way of the other kids so he wouldn't get jumped on. And where are these kids' parents? Why didn't hey notice that my child wasn't getting a chance to play!

> **That day Nicholas taught me about patience, acceptance, and unconditional love. He really did seem to enjoy himself.**

Deep down, I know these are my feelings because I am his mother and I try to keep my feelings and emotions under control. But apparently I have a jealous streak. I have to remind myself that I'm on a journey and that Nicholas will always be discipling me. That day Nicholas taught me about patience, acceptance, and unconditional love. He really did seem to enjoy himself. He liked being in the presence of other kids—just playing without the assistance and interference of his mom.

What I had to realize was that he is comfortable with who he is. The other kids didn't look at him strangely and none of them even asked why he wasn't jumping. They jus played. And on that day he was normal, even though his overprotective mom was jealous.

"Yes you have been with me from birth; from my mothers womb you have cared for me. No wonder I am always praising you! My life is an example to many, because you have been my strength and protection. That is why I can never stop praising you? I declare your glory all day long."
Psalm 71:6-8 (NLT)

Uncertainty in my world is wondering how many limitations Nicholas will have. I fear for his future. I know that as long as he is with me and I am with him, then I will do my best to compensate in the areas where he is not strong. However, the "what if's" are very scary.

My biggest fear is that I don't know how he will handle life without me. How do I teach him that? I am his caretaker and biggest advocate. Helen Featherstone states it best in her book <u>A Difference in the Family</u>,

"A child's disability raises the specter of his parents' old age, declining strength, and death.

Even normal children exact a heavy commitment of time, energy, and emotion. But ordinary parenting follows a natural cycle that respects our morality. When parents are young and healthy and energetic, children require vast amounts of exhausting physical care. As both grow older, this demand tapers off, and eventually the children grow independent. Parents hope and expect that by the time they die, their sons and daughters will no longer need overseeing judgment or care. A sever disability disrupts this natural order, extending a child's dependence beyond a parents strength, health, even lifetime. A disabled child forces parents to think of their old age in ugly, dismal terms."

Prior to one Christmas, while shopping in a local toy store, I noticed a group of adults who were following the direction of a gentleman who was obviously their caretaker. I immediately decided that they were probably from a group home. Right away I spotted that one of them had Down syndrome. I began to think that although I want Nicholas to be as independent as possible, I didn't want him to live and shop with strangers.

For several days after seeing the group I really

struggled with how I am raising my children. I realized that my plan is to put my responsibilities for Nicholas off on his sisters. I had to face the question of am I trying to have my girls live an abnormal life, in order to take care of their brother. Honestly, even today, my answer is yes.

> I will admit, I selfishly want the girls to make a place for Nicholas in their lives and in their homes.

People often talk about twins having a special connection. Nicholas' twin sister has the strongest personality of my children. As of right now, I pray that she will always have a special connection to him that keeps her feeling like she doesn't want him too far away from her. I want her to always take care of her brother, even though he is not her responsibility.

His older sister has my nurturing, loving, and vulnerable traits. She likes learning family traditions and she remembers everything. I pray that she will keep the three of them tightly connected. I will admit, I selfishly want the girls to make a place for Nicholas in their lives and in their homes. I want them to marry and build a family but with the understanding that their husbands must accept their brother. I know that is selfish, but it's my truth.

> *"Don't worry about anything; instead, pray about everything. Tell God what you need, and thank Him for all that He has done."*
> Philippians 4:6 (NLT)

Tell God. I thought I knew how to pray, until I met Nicholas. Throughout my life there have been many situations, failures, and hardships that caused me to pray. Sometimes I prayed in the moment. Sometimes I prayed for a few days. And sometimes I prayed for months or years over a situation.

When I first laid eyes on my son, my prayer life with God changed in an instant. Praying for the well-being, or better yet the life of my newborn baby, took my prayers to a new level. Nicholas has taught me the importance of daily communication with God.

Having a child with any diagnosis gives you more issues to consider as a parent. There are so many things that I took for granted until Nicholas entered my life. Like climbing steps for instance—I don't think twice when I see his twin sister go up and down the stairs to her bedroom. But when Nicholas heads towards those same stairs, I find myself holding my breath, or standing a little closer to the steps (inconspicuously of course), just in case he needs help. Or when he wants to slide down off the bed, or stand up to shower, or play with other children.

Because my reality is that in an instant things can quickly go in a negative direction, I also find myself praying for the future of all my children more. I pray that they will be close, having heart strings that can't be broken from each other. I pray that they take a little extra precaution when it comes to their brother. When I'm old, I just don't want to be left wondering, "But what about Nic?"

The website allaboutprayer.org says that prayer is simply talking to God. When I consider the prayers I'm familiar with, I think of daily prayers, intercessory prayers, and The Lord's Prayer just to name a few. In August of 2009 when I knew that Nicholas was going in for his first open heart surgery, I named my own new prayer, "A Mother's Prayer."

My daily prayers had always consisted of a quick morning prayer that may have lasted all of five minutes. The family prayers were reserved for bedtime. Intercessory prayers were just quick prayers that God would bless the sick and needy. And The Lord's Prayer was something I could recite at will.

However, after Nicholas entered my life, all of my prayers changed. Now, I don't talk at God, I have conversations with Him. My daily prayers are truly daily—all day. I start early in the morning before my household awakes and they continue into the night after everyone has gone back to sleep. There is not a waking moment that I am not concerned about my children and their safety. I pray that whomever they come in contact with has their best interest at heart.

> **I will admit that I talk to God all day on the behalf of Nicholas, sometimes to the point that I have to go back and say "Ditto for his sisters!"**

My prayers for Nicholas are that I am making the right decisions on his behalf. I pray that he continues to be verbal and that his speech is understood and that in those times when he is not understood that it doesn't result in him facing pain or hurt feelings. I will admit that I talk to God all day on the behalf of Nicholas, sometimes to the point that I have to go back and say "Ditto for his sisters!" Then I feel as though I have slighted my girls, and the whole prayer process starts again on their behalf. Sometimes I think God gives me what I ask for because I've gotten on His nerves!

My family prayers have changed as well. I make sure we pray and praise God together as a family unit. We talk about God and I point out when God has moved in the lives of our family and our friends, especially those that we have met on this journey. We pray for other families who are in need of God's divine intervention. We even talk about death.

My girls understand that sometimes God has to heal children with His own hands and that's why they have to go into an eternal sleep. I get other family members and close friends involved in prayer when we are facing "big" issues. I don't mind shedding tears in front of my children as I thank God for what He has already done in our lives and the extra special blessings He has given Nicholas. We love to sing praises unto God and express our happiness together. And we love going to church, especially Nicholas.

Concerning my intercessory prayers…the ones that I used to offer as a by the way type of prayer…now I spend some serious time in this arena. Never before had I thought about sick babies, until God gave me one. Somehow I always believed that illness was reserved for old people. It is embarrassing to admit that I thought all sick babies and children were only at St. Jude's Hospital. I honestly never thought beyond their commercials. Never did I imagine babies having broken hearts and genetic abnormalities.

But once I was introduced to the Special Needs Community…my life and prayer life has changed forever. I remember sitting in the hospital room feeling sorry for my little boy, while looking over at his roommate –alone, and with his tiny limbs growing from the wrong areas of his body. That situation made me reevaluate my and feelings. Even though my child had a serious condition, he was doing much better than most of the other babies in the unit. It taught me not to be selfish in my prayers, but to truly pray for other children and their families.

I remember my first true intercessory prayer was for a baby whose parents had walked away before he was 48 hours old – before his open heart surgery that had to take place in the hospital room, because he was too fragile to be physically moved to an operating room. I remember praying for a little guy who needed a kidney transplant, as his parents, grandparents, aunts and uncles were being tested to see if they were a match. Now, I find myself praying especially praying for the mothers who face the unknown…those just waiting to hear what's wrong.

I have prayed earnestly that I am never in the shoes of those mothers that have had to bury their babies. But

I pray heartily that they gain a little peace as their baby's transition. Never before had I really known how to pray for others, until I met a new community of people…all because of Nicholas, my little disciple.

> I must admit handing my barely 10 pound baby boy over to a team of scrub clad strangers has been the hardest moment ever!

"In my desperation I prayed, and the Lord listened; He saved me from all my troubles."
Psalms 34:6 (NLT)

Considering all the hurt, heartache, and failures that have occurred in my life, I must admit handing my barely 10 pound baby boy over to a team of scrub clad strangers has been the hardest moment ever! And then to think --- they're going to work on his heart. Nic's heart.

I remember his surgeon, Dr. Eric Mendeloff, telling me that Nic's heart was about the size of a walnut and that he was going to turn if off so he could fix it—then he'd start it back up! I sat there thinking, Is that possible? The heart, God's masterpiece, so delicate, so intricate, how can this doctor just turn it off and back on?

On the day of surgery I truly prayed. I prayed that God would send Nicholas some guardian angels that would surround his bedside. I wanted those angels to comfort him as he literally faced the fight for his life. I prayed for every hand that touched my son and for all the instruments the workers would use to touch my baby. I prayed for the custodian who was responsible for cleaning and sterilizing the area before everyone arrived. I prayed for good weather so there wasn't a possibility of a power outage. I prayed that the bypass machine was in good working condition, so it properly fooled his body into thinking the heart was still "turned on."

Most of all I prayed for "Dr. M". I prayed that he was well rested and that if he felt weak God would give him strength to perform the 4 hour surgery my baby so desperately needed. I prayed that he wouldn't grow weak or fatigued. I prayed that he would remember the proper steps to be taken in order to repair Nicholas' heart, and that he would make excellent judgment calls if needed. And I most happily report that my prayers were answered by God. Nicholas came through surgery like a Warrior.

"Rejoice in our confident hope. Be patient in trouble,

and keep on praying."
Romans 12:12 (NLT)

I've learned that it is easy for us to have a conversation with God in good times, when we have all the answers on our own. But when things are going bad and we cannot fix our own problems we can cry out to God and we can hang on to His promises!

God should be our solution in times of trouble. Our challenge is that when things are going well and our challenge has passed, we cannot relax our prayer life. God enjoys that intimate time with us; we should not stop including Him in our easy times---because He is concerned even then.

Nicholas has taught me that I must be in constant communication with God. If I'm not in a storm, then I need to be thanking Him for bringing me through with my sanity. My praise needs to continue so I'm prepared for the next storm. I've heard older church mothers call it "storing up some prayers" and "sending up timber."

I've learned that as I physically prepare Nicholas for his operations, that I must spiritually prepare him as well. WE say prayers, I pray out loud with him often. In difficult times I have been taught to maintain my relationship with God...thank you Nicholas.

> *"But in my distress I cried out to the Lord; yes, I prayed to my God for help. He heard me from His sanctuary; my cry to Him reached His ears."*
> Psalm 18:6 (NLT)

> **I recall being angry with God because He had not chosen to miraculously heal my baby so he could go home with me and his twin sister.**

Thinking back to the day I checked out of the hospital after having my twins, I could only take the healthy twin sister home. On that I day I just cried. I have experienced death of loved ones, divorce, failed friendships, and major meltdowns---but leaving Nicholas behind at the hospital hurt to my inner most being.

I remember having this overwhelming feeling that he would think I had abandoned him, whereas in reality, it was the first time I had left his bedside for any length of time. I recall being angry with God because He had not chosen to miraculously heal my baby so he could go home with me and his twin sister. I was angry with the doctors because it seemed like every time I spoke with them, they had another concern or diagnosis that would surely keep my Nicholas in the hospital even longer. And I was extremely mad at my mother because she told me to stop crying and feeling sorry for myself. How dare she say that to me and I was leaving a piece of my heart lying on a bed.

Nobody, including God, had done or said anything I wanted to hear. I've shed many tears, tears of sadness, fear, heartache, and ultimately joy. I have cried and not known it until I felt the wetness on my clothes. I would cry every time I entered Nicholas' hospital room with those bells and whistles sounding off – crying because I was happy he had good stats, or crying because it would seem like he was struggling to maintain. I once heard someone say that tears are soul cleansers. If that is true, my should must be awfully clean.

Before Nicholas was born, when I received the diagnosis that his heart wasn't developing properly, it brought forth an abundance of tears – tears, due to the unknown. Of course I thought about the worse case scenario. Then the cardiologist told me that this type of defect is found primarily in children who also have Down syndrome.

At that moment of reality, tears began to flow. I felt like she had just taken a sledge hammer and caved it into the middle of my chest. Surely, she was mistaken.

I couldn't bring myself to ask a question, or to make a comment. Thank God my god sister had met me at that appointment, because she asked every question that I was supposed to ask.

I was in a state of shock, and I could not stop crying while wondering would my baby survive. I tried to convince myself that God loved my baby more than I did, but that was even a challenge.

The first few months of life were pretty hard on Nicholas. His body had to learn how to function on its own, without the help of my womb. I was so sad that he couldn't keep his body temperature regulated. I knew that I was anemic and I wondered if I had passed that off to him also. There my little baby lay in bed with a heat lamp over him…baking.

I wanted the nurse to wrap my sweet baby up in a warm blanket and let me hold him and spoil him. I even cried because in my mind he was uncomfortable just lying in bed. I became extremely overwhelmed with thinking he didn't know his Momma was right there beside him. I felt like was missing out on what was normal. I just wanted him to be normal.

I was told by the hospital staff of ALL the issues he'd probably face. It was explained to me that for his benefit I couldn't hold him at certain times—but he was still my baby. Just a little baby that needed his Momma to hold him and sing him lullabies. I was sad that he was missing story time and tummy time with his twin sister. Even though I knew he was receiving the best care in the world. My heart just hurt because there wasn't anything I could do to take all his illnesses away.

> **Yet Nicholas has taught me that God loves both of us more than I can ever imagine. God knows every tear that I have shed.**

"Then Jesus wept. The people who were standing nearby said, "See how much He loved him!"
John 11:35-36 (NLT)

When I look into Nicholas' little round face, I see how much God loves me. He loves me so much that He trusts me to raise Nicholas. But my tears are still here 4 years later. I still cry when Nicholas doesn't understand simple commands or doesn't know how to handle various situations.

Yet Nicholas has taught me that God loves both of us more than I can ever imagine. God knows every tear that I have shed. The happy tears I silently cry when he meets a milestone, when he "gets it." But God also hears the wailing tears I shed when I have no idea how long a doctor is going to require me to hold Nic down on an examination table. God knows the tears I cry when I have to give overnight feedings because he hasn't gained enough muscle tone to drink or eat. God sees the tears I shed when I watch Nicholas play with other kids his age and they tower over him in height and act like they don't see him. By knowing that even Jesus wept with His friends Mary and Martha about their brother Lazarus, I know He cares enough for me that He also has compassion for me and my broken baby.

"So I recommend having fun, because there is nothing better for people in this world than to eat, drink, and enjoy life. That way they will experience some happiness along with all the hard work God gives them under the sun."
Ecclesiastes 8:15 (NLT)

Nicholas makes me reflect on the present time and to find happiness in it. So many times we consider happiness based upon possessions. Nicholas has taught me that happiness can be displayed in simply sitting down.

Nic always tries to keep up with his twin sister. One evening we were headed to the kitchen table for dinner and he decided to get a step and try getting into his seat on his own. Due to us having higher than normal chairs and tables in that area, plus having a booster seat strapped to the chair—I was afraid for him to attempt this alone. All I could think about is he's going to fall and bump his head, or slip and hit his chin on the table. However the accident happens—it's going to be bad and we're surely heading to the hospital!

However, I took a chance and stood back, inconspicuously watching ever move he made. I watched as he carried the step over to the table near his seat, positioned it just right so he could hold on to the chair and the table at the same time. After getting some good footing he raised his little leg up and knelt into the booster seat, swiveled around, sat down, raised hi hands and said "Tah-Dah, I did it!"

He was so proud of his accomplishment Yes, I held my breath and prayed he wouldn't fail again. I considered how I would encourage him if he decided to let his fears get the best of him and give up before getting into his seat. Sometimes I'm a cheerleader, sometimes I'm a coach, and sometimes I'm a medic, but in all those times---I'm a Mom, and seeing my child succeed fills my heart with joy.

As I look back over my life until this point, I can remember so many things that I thought made me happy. Since having children, I've learned to appreciate and be happy with the small stuff. Society has urged us into thinking that the more tangible items we possess, the happier we will be.

> The ultimate happiness for me is hearing Nicholas sing praise and worship songs that he has learned from Sunday morning service while playing his tambourine.

And I must admit that I had fallen into that thought process.

However, now, I know better. Now, I'm happy just to hear my child call my name, and I know he truly recognizes who I am. Happiness these days is watching him build up his confidence enough to walk along side other children who we consider typical. Happiness is watching Nicholas pick up a book and pretend to read, with every page ending in "Amen." Happiness is watching him and his sister's dance with Mickey Mouse and the gang while singing along with the Clubhouse Song.

But happiness is also found when he takes his meds by mouth without choking and crying or ultimately going into a full blown meltdown and vomiting session. Happiness is making it through a night without any alarms ringing and being awakened with fear. Selfishly, happiness is seeing Nicholas achieve tasks that some children struggle with. It validates his normalcy…if only for that moment.

The ultimate happiness for me is hearing Nicholas sing praise and worship songs that he has learned from Sunday morning service while playing his tambourine. I've learned that God doesn't have to bless you with a perfectly healthy child in order to bless you. When I think about it, there is nothing I would change about Nicholas' personality, or his development. I would gladly change his health conditions for the better and the world's perception of what's considered "normal."

NOTES

Part Four: A Better Understanding

So God has given both His promise and His oath. These two things are unchangeable because it is impossible for God to lie. Therefore, we who have fled to Him for refuge can have great confidence as we hold to the hope that lies before us. This hope is a strong and trustworthy anchor for our souls. It leads us through the curtain into God's inner sanctuary.
Hebrews 6:18-19 (NLT)

A disability is a physical or mental condition that limits a person's movements, senses, or activities; a disadvantage or handicap, especially one imposed or recognized by the law. A disability may be physical, cognitive, mental, sensory, emotional, and developmental or some combination of these. A disability may be present from birth, or occur during a person's lifetime. Thus, disability is a complex phenomenon, reflecting an interaction between features of a person's body and features of the society in which he or she lives." (WIKIPEDIA)

> **I've had to learn to accept Nicholas' obstacles as a result of his genetic differences. Thinking that way doesn't make it easier, just easier to accept.**

One of the hardest things for me to accept is that my son has a disability called Down syndrome. Unfortunately, a lot of things are a struggle for him. I've always looked at my own struggles as obstacles I need to overcome. So I've had to learn to accept Nicholas' obstacles as a result of his genetic differences. Thinking that way doesn't make it easier, just easier to accept.

I would like to share some facts about Down

syndrome from the National Down syndrome Society:
- Down syndrome is the most commonly occurring genetic condition. There are more than 400,000 people living with Down syndrome in the United States. One in every 691 babies in the U.S. is born with Down syndrome.
- The incidents of births of children with Down syndrome increases with the age of the mother. But due to higher fertility rates in younger women, 80% of children with Down syndrome are born to women under 35 years of age.
- People with Down syndrome have an increased risk for certain medical conditions such as heart defects, respiratory, and hearing problems, Alzheimer's disease, childhood leukemia, and thyroid conditions. Many of these conditions are now treatable, so most people with Down syndrome lead healthy lives.
- All people with Down syndrome experience cognitive delays, but the effect is usually mild to moderate and is not indicative of the many strengths and talents that each individual possesses.
- While it is still clinically acceptable to say "mental retardation," you should use the more

socially acceptable "intellectual disability" or "cognitive disability." NDSS strongly condemns the use of the word "retarded" in any derogatory context. Using this word is hurtful and suggests that people with disabilities are not competent.
- Individuals with Down syndrome are becoming increasingly integrated into society and community organizations, such as school, health care systems, work offices, and social and recreational activities.

One of my biggest pet peeves is to hear someone say, "He is Downs." No he isn't! Dr. John Langdon Down, is "Down's." Down syndrome is named after this English doctor because he was the first person to distinguish Down syndrome from other conditions by noting common features associated with it. Most people don't know that this syndrome is simply named for the man who first described it.

Another fact that is looked over is that Dr. Jerome Lejeune discovered that Down syndrome is a genetic disorder whereby a person has three copies of Chromosome 21 instead of two. Chromosomes are the structures in cells that contain the genes. It is important to know that Down syndrome has nothing to do with race, nationality, socioeconomic status, religion, or anything the mother or father did during pregnancy. (GLOBAL)

Down syndrome means that my baby boy has a genetic condition. Instead of having two copies of the 21st chromosome (one from Mom and one from Dad), he got an extra one from somebody. And since science cannot determine which one of us gave it to him "I" choose to believe it came from God's DNA.

> ...since science cannot determine which one of us gave it to him "I" choose to believe it came from God's DNA.

Studies say that this extra chromosome will affect his life forever and make his appearance slightly different from others. With that definition, how could it not be God's chromosome? Some other commonalities are a flattened bridge of the nose, upward slanting eyes, a short neck, the back of the head is flat, broad short hands with a single crease in the palm, short fingers, protruding tongue, excessive flexibility, and a wide gap between the first and second toes.

Of course not everybody with Down syndrome has these same differences, but these differences occur together often enough to be considered characteristics of Down syndrome. Nicholas has each of those characteristics.

The MAYO Clinic advises that
> Infants with Down syndrome may be of average size (when born), but typically they grow slowly and remain shorter than children of similar age. In general, developmental milestones, such as sitting and crawling, occur at about twice the age of children without impairment. Children with Down syndrome also have some degree of mental retardation, most often in the mild to moderate range.

When I discussed these with my Mom, she began to reflect on family members who have the same characteristics. She advised me that my Great Grandmothers eyes slanted, a Great Aunt had a big gap between her first two toes (and so do I), and several of us protrude our tongues while in deep thought (again I fall into that category). So basically in her mind Nicholas inherited most of his characteristics. That conversation was quite funny!

As a parent, especially a mother, we wonder if it is our fault that our child is suffering. When my husband and I met with the genetic counselor she advised that typically children get one gene from each parent, however in Nic's situation he got an extra gene from one of us. His Dad immediately replied with, "Well, which one of us gave him that gene?"

My heart sunk. I immediately felt like he wanted to blame me for our son having this label. The counselor must have noticed the pain in my eyes and hurt on my face because she immediately responded with "we do not know—science hasn't figured that out."

What we do know is that people with Down syndrome and many other diagnosed disabilities have a lot to offer. Currently the life span of a person with Down syndrome is around 60 years. In 1983, the average lifespan was 25 years. It is believed that this dramatic increase is due to society not expecting people with disabilities to be institutionalized but to function in society.

I personally believe that through faith, prayer, and an appropriate education Nicholas and others can and will lead pretty normal lives. Thankfully in the late 1970's housing institutions began to close down, because people with Down syndrome were expected to live at home enjoying the same fundamental human rights as others. I cannot imagine Nicholas not living at home with our family. He offers so much as he interacts in daily activities. Yes, some days can be quite challenging. Yes, there are behavioral, emotional, and physical challenges that I have to deal with—but by the Grace of God—it works out for our good.

"And we know that God causes everything to work together for the good of those who love God and are called according to His purpose for them."
Romans 8:28 (NLT)

When I say appropriate education I mean for the person and the parent or guardian. I have found that early detection of other medical conditions was very helpful on our journey.

For instance, with Down syndrome, the appropriate physical, occupational, and speech therapies in the early stages of life have proven to make a major difference in their development. Yes, it is heartbreaking to hear that your child is not "typical/normal." However, it is important for their future that you love them enough to make their success your first priority.

Every family is unique and some developments are more important to one family than to another. For example, it is very important to me that Nicholas is able to communicate on a level were the majority of people can understand him. For a child with Down syndrome to be nonverbal is not unlikely. I just didn't want that to be our situation. I chose to read to him a lot and play music to sing to and make him "use his words." I would often say "Nic, use your words!"

> **We had a wonderful therapist who made me understand the importance of him communicating versus talking.**

We had a wonderful therapist who made me understand the importance of him communicating versus talking. She taught us how to sign the words that were important in our daily interaction. She also taught me signs/signals for immediate commands, such as a signal for him to immediately stop doing anything that could cause harm to himself.

This was so important to me because I worried about potential danger while in the kitchen, around stairs, outside, etc. An additional benefit for Nicholas is that his sisters expected him to talk to them. Now, there is a downside—because I focused so strongly in those areas, I didn't focus in other areas as I wish I would have, such as his eating habits and potty training.

I remember sitting in the therapy lobby waiting for

Nicholas to be called for his session and I saw a little boy who looked to be near Nic's age and also having Down syndrome, gesture to his Dad that he needed to go to the restroom. I was amazed! I began to think how much easier my life would be if Nic was potty trained. No more diaper bags, no more purchasing pampers and wipes and butt paste...No more embarrassment at daycare when he has to be taken away to be changed while the other boys head to the restroom...Then just moments later the therapist stood at the door and called for Nicholas. He said, "bye-bye Mommy, I see you later,"

Then the Dad of the other little boy whom I had been admiring looked over and said to me, I would give anything for my son to talk to me and call me Daddy." Immediately I stopped feeling sorry for myself and we exchanged stories and ideas on potty training and talking. I thanked God for that encounter. He allowed me to be reassured that all children don't learn the same things at the same times—no matter their diagnosis.

Today, as I sit and write, my children are enjoying a fun-filled day at The State Fair in Dallas. I'm so glad that expectation and acceptance of people with Special Needs has changed. I cannot imagine Nicholas not being able to go out to enjoy rides, shows, and water parks with his sisters. I cannot imagine a parent having to leave their child behind because society thinks they shouldn't interact with everyone. Thank God for the shift.

Even with the many advances we still have a long way to go. The Global Down Syndrome Foundation reports that despite the 1980's legislation, there are still some doctors who believe a person with Down syndrome should be denied life-saving procedures. We must advocate for our children, whatever the disability. We must make sure we have accurate, detailed, and informative information available for future generations.

"Teach those who are rich in this world not to be proud and not to trust in their money, which is so unreliable. Their trust should be in God, who richly gives us all we need for our enjoyment. Tell them to use their money to do good. They should be rich in good works and generous to those in need, always being ready to share with others. By doing this they will be storing up their treasure as a good foundation for the future so that they may experience true life."
1Timothy 6:17-19 (NLT)

The Other Issue…
One of the dominating issues with Down syndrome is

that it's often coupled with a congenital heart defect. With a congenital heart defect, a part of the heart does not form properly before birth. This changes the normal operations and flow of blood through the heart. There are over 35 types of congenital heart defect's. Some are simple, others are more complex. They include combinations of simple defects, problems with the location of blood vessels leading to and from the heart, and more serious problems with how the heart develops. (National Heart Lung and Blood Institute)

> **There are over 35 types of congenital heart defect's. Some are simple, others are more complex.**

I would like to share a few congenital heart defect facts from Heartwaves.org:
- congenital heart defect are the #1 birth defect worldwide.
- Nearly twice as many children die from congenital heart defect in the U.S. each year as from all forms of childhood cancers combined, yet funding for pediatric cancer research is five times higher than funding for congenital heart defect.
- Each year in the U.S. approximately 4,000 babies (under one year old) will not live to

celebrate their first birthday.
- The cost for inpatient surgery to repair congenital heart defect exceeds $2.2 billion a years.
- The American Heart Association directs only $0.30 of every dollar donated toward research. The remainder goes toward administration, education, and fund raising efforts. Of the $0.30 that goes toward research only $0.01 goes toward pediatric cardiology for congenital heart defects.
- It is a proven fact that the earlier a congenital heart defect is detected and treated', the more likely it is the affected child will survive and have fewer long term health complications.

The form of congenital heart defect that my son has is Complete/Full Atrioventricular Canal Defect (AV Canal). It is a combination of several abnormalities that causes a large hole between the chambers of the heart and causes problems with the valves that regulate blood flow in the heart.

In a normal heart, the left side of the heart pumps blood to the body, and the right side of the heart pumps blood to the lungs. However, in a child with AV Canal defect, blood can travel across the holes from the left of the heart chambers over to the right and out into the lungs. The extra blood that is pumped into the lungs makes the heart and the lungs work harder and the lungs become congested.

This is a very common type of heart defect in children with Down syndrome. This defect causes the infant to breathe harder and faster than normal, and causes problems with feeding. Thankfully, AV Canal defect can be repaired through open-heart surgery.

This defect cannot close on its own or with medication, it must be repaired. Because of the strain it puts on the heart, the repair needs to happen during infancy. According to heart.org:
> During the operation, the surgeon closes the large hole with one or two patches. Later the patch will become a permanent part of the heart as the heart's lining grows over it. The surgeon also divides the single valve between the heart's upper and lower chambers and makes two separate valves. These will be made as close to normal valves as possible.

When Nicholas was born, he weighed 6lbs and 4oz. The cardiologist advised that she preferred him to be at least 10 pounds before undergoing the surgery to repair his heart. With the combination of low muscle tone (which also affects mouth muscles), poor feeding, and poor weight gain; it took every bit of five months for him to gain weight. These set backs forced him to have a feeding tube inserted around a week old to help his feeding efforts. And unfortunately after three months he completely stopped sucking a bottle.

> **I remember thinking that since God knew Nic's heart would be broken, He blessed him with Down syndrome so he would have an advantage during recovery.**

That's when I was truly faced with how weak his heart was—he was too weak to eat. Additionally, with his heart working so hard just to sustain life, he didn't develop his motor skills. As his sister had tummy time I'd position him with her, but Nicholas would just lay there looking around.

It seemed like set back after set back. But God still gave me comfort even during those times. I read somewhere and later had a nurse to share with me that with certain types of Heart Defects, people with Down syndrome are more likely than their typical counterparts to recover and recover quickly.

I remember thinking that since God knew Nic's heart

would be broken, He blessed him with Down syndrome so he would have an advantage during recovery.

For most congenital heart defect families, there is a continued fear that you live with---"we have to go back in to fix something else." It is important to note that any child's progress will be affected by illnesses and hospitalizations. As with Nicholas, other health issues ended up being a top priority, rather than motor skill development.

I remember an older church mother advising me not to even "expect" much until Nicholas had fully recovered from his heart surgery. That ended up being some very valuable advice. I had to remember that my baby came into this world with a major setback. In the words of my mother, "Nicholas has gone through more in the first year of his life than some of us will experience in a lifetime."

It is also helpful to remember that some children with the same diagnoses may progress slower than their counterpart, but that is true with typical children as well. I would also like to believe that the family environment plays a major role in development. As a family, we have expectations of each other. And Nicholas is not excluded. Everyone knows that he may not progress at the same rate as his twin sister, but will still require him to make a diligent effort.

All of my children have outgoing personalities and they are socialites. Nicholas loves to mimic people that he loves. He loves his Pastor. Nicholas holds "play church" at home with his sisters. He serves as the usher, choir, deacon, and preacher. He makes his sisters play with him—he shows them where to sit, tells them what to sing, then he prays followed by putting on his bathrobe and grabbing anything that can improvise for a microphone and he starts preaching.

Even when we attend our actual church services, he enters boldly, often with his tambourine in hand, ready for praise and worship. He's not the kid that falls asleep in church. He's wide awake and paying attention. I've grown used to this behavior, but I am still intrigued by it. I'm grateful for that Designer "God" gene in Nicholas.

The final diagnosis Nicholas received was Hirschsprung's disease. This is a congenital disease and results from missing nerves in a part or the entire colon, making them unable to have a bowel movement.

As a baby develops in the mother's womb, bundles of

nerve cells normally begin to form between the muscle layers along the length of the colon. This process begins at the top of the colon and ends at the rectum.

In children who have Hirschsprung's disease, the nerve-growing process fails to finish. Most commonly, it affects the last segment of the colon.

> **Hate is a strong word. There are only a few things that I hate. Hirschsprung's Disease is one of them.**

The treatment for this is to surgically bypass or remove the diseased portion of the colon. This was the case with Nicholas.

Hate is a strong word. There are only a few things that I hate. Hirschsprung's Disease is one of them. This condition has given Nicholas more problems than any other diagnosis.

Immediately following giving birth to him and his sister, I had some personal complications. Because I had problems with my oldest child, I had already planned that my mother would be with Nicholas in the event I could not.

Mom shared with me that Nicholas didn't want to

take a bottle and the nurse demonstrated some helpful tips to encourage his sucking. We were happy that his sucking had finally kicked in by the night fall of the first day. We were thankful that his heart was producing enough energy and strength for him to eat on his own.

But as hours passed, as days passed, he was not passing stool. Then the vicious cycle of taking the bottle away, poking, prodding, X-rays, biopsies and enemas would begin – not to mention I couldn't even hold him because he had to stay under the heat lamp in his bed in order to have a healthy body temperature.

Thinking back, I can remember that his condition was not nearly as traumatic as his roommates and neighbors, but in the moment---my heart was wrenching. My baby couldn't catch a break.

After a couple days of "let's see if we can fix this without surgery" we found out that surgery was indeed necessary. Before a week old Nicholas was given a colostomy. A colostomy is a surgical procedure in which a stoma is formed by drawing the healthy end of the large intestine or colon through an incision in the anterior abdominal wall and suturing it into place. This opening, in conjunction with the attached stoma appliance, provides an alternative channel for feces to leave the body. It may be reversible or irreversible depending on the circumstances. (Wikipedia)

I was absolutely not prepared for this. It was hard for me to imagine my little baby, whose heart was already broken, going in for surgery at just a few days old. But I knew he was in pain and without surgery it would only get worse.

Thankfully after the surgery he was not in pain anymore. But accepting the fact that Nicholas had a colostomy was a different issue. Sticking a bag on my baby's belly to catch his waste broke my heart. There was nothing normal about this. Not knowing if it would last a lifetime was a constant worry. I wondered how I would explain this to him, how would his peers treat him, what would his sisters say—and why him?

God was so faithful to me during this time. The colostomy was only a big deal to me. The nurses taught me how to change his bag, and gave me pointers on making the bag stick better to his skin. Once I got the hang of it, my bags stayed on longer than theirs. One nurse even took the time to make a chart in his room to keep score! Me vs. the nurses. For them to make a game out of whose bag stays on the longest made accepting yet another difference a little easier for me.

"So I recommend having fun, because there is nothing better for people in this world than to eat, drink, and enjoy life. That way they will experience some happiness along with all the hard work God gives them under the sun."
Ecclesiastes 8:15 (NLT)

The combination of his various diagnoses forced Nicholas to spend the first 42 days of his life in the NICU of Medical City Children's Hospital of Dallas, Texas. As if the blessing of my sweet Nicholas wasn't enough, God gave me another memorable gift—Nicholas' release date was on Easter Sunday morning. This was following my "in house training" to prepare to go home.

The rules said that I had to spend a few days, around the clock, caring for Nicholas, doing all the things that I would need to do for him once we got home. The nurses made sure I properly drew and gave meds, tube feedings were administered properly, and that I could administer breathing treatments correctly. I would have to be able to recognize if his heart would begin to fail and how to administer infant CPR.

That Easter Sunday was the last day that I was supposed to fulfill my obligation to prove that I could care for Nicholas on my own. That Sunday would also be the first time that my oldest daughter Nadia would perform in a program. I asked the doctor on call for special permission to leave for a few hours so that I could attend church with her.

While at church, during altar prayer, my cell phone rang. I had it on vibrate, but when I saw that it was the hospital phone number…my heart sunk. As the church prayers ended, my personal prayers got stronger. I could not imagine any good reason that the hospital was calling me. Did something happen unexpectedly? Had I done something wrong with meds before I left? Was Nicholas still alive? I called the number back, and to my surprise the nurse said, "Nicholas is being released today. Come pick up your baby." I ran back into the sanctuary to share the wonderful news—Nicholas was coming home!

"In times of trouble, may the Lord answer your cry. May the name of the God of Jacob keep you safe from all harm. May He send you help from His sanctuary and strengthen you from Jerusalem. May He remember all your gifts and look favorably on your burnt offerings. May He grant your heart's desires and make all your plans succeed. May we shout for joy when we hear of your victory and raise a victory banner in the name of our God. May the Lord answer all your prayers."
                    Psalm 20:1-5 (NLT)

NOTES

Part Five: Christian Parenting

Trust in the Lord with all your heart; do not depend on your own understanding. Seek His will in all you do, and He will show you which path to take.
Proverbs 3:5-6 (NLT)

I often hear that "God gives special children to special parents."

In our case, God chose to give Nicholas to a special family, extended family, and close friends who prove to be a great asset for him. Another popular phrase from the educational arena is, "It takes a village to raise a child."

> ...raising a child is the responsibility of everyone who is connected to that child from the home, the church, the school, and the community.

The implication is that raising a child is the responsibility of everyone who is connected to that child from the home, the church, the school, and the community. I encourage parents to build a village.

I have learned to depend on my "village people." They help me, from providing free childcare to paying medical expenses. They pray with me and for me. And because we strive to live by the same Christian beliefs and moral guidelines, I can trust them to treat my children the same way they would treat their own.

In the beginning I thought "I" had to do everything for Nicholas. I believed that if I didn't do everything for him then I was being a bad mother. I felt like no one else would understand his cry, or recognize his grimaces, or understand his form of sign language…especially during the time he was non verbal. I thought that I was the only person who could give his meds correctly, hook up the feeding pump, and change his colostomy bag to make it stick.

I was his mother. These were my duties. I wanted to make sure this special little boy that God trusted me with did not suffer as a result of something I didn't do for him. I watched his every move. Even when he was asleep. I felt like if something were to happen to him, I could never forgive myself, nor would God and anybody else forgive me.

I just didn't realize that I was running myself down. I didn't share the fact that it hurt my feelings not to have a happy story to share about the labor and birth of my new babies. Instead, I was worried about the health of my son, and if his heart was going to be strong enough to sustain him until it could be repaired.

However, I did find comfort in other parents in the NICU, especially, other mothers. I didn't have to explain the look of fear on my face, because they understood and shared my same look. They just knew.

They could relate to me jumping every time a monitor would ring out—just praying that it wasn't my child having the problem. Even though our children may have had different diagnoses, we shared a common bond that did not have to be verbalized.

> *"Years passed, and the king of Egypt died. But the Israelites continued to groan under their burden of slavery. They cried out for help, and their cry rose up to God. God heard their groaning, and He remembered His covenant promise to Abraham, Isaac, and Jacob. He looked down on the people of Israel and knew it was time to act."*
> Exodus 2:23-25 (NLT)

All parents have certain expectations of their children. I choose not to expect anything less of Nicholas than I do from his twin sister. However, I do understand that he may not accomplish a task or master a skill as quickly as she does. But not expecting him to do so is simply not acceptable.

I remember that at two years old his twin Nia could put on her own shoes. Nicholas didn't accomplish that goal until he was four—but he did it. And I celebrated his accomplishment just as jubilantly as I had celebrated two years before.

I've learned that things may not always go the way I think they should, or the way the doctors and therapists tell me they will. Nicholas has taught me to slow down and enjoy seeing God's hand in simple everyday things, to enjoy and appreciate things that I used to take for granted.

> **I've learned to consult God even if it's something that I think I can handle. I've learned that consulting God first makes everything go a little smoother.**

I've learned to consult God even if it's something that I think I can handle. I've learned that consulting God first makes everything go a little smoother.

Parenting has taught me to approach timelines and deadlines differently, especially when your child has limitations. Generally a "special" parent is just happy when our child finally "gets it"—whatever the goal is. This is why we set goals without deadlines and celebrate each small step that it takes to reach it.

Although every child is unique and every family is different, we share common concerns that bond us together. We worry about our child's acceptance in our family, the school, and the community. We plan for an uncertain future, and we try to set appropriate goals.

The best advice I can give another parent of a child with special needs is to be flexible, compassionate, stubborn, and resilient. In the Christian's reality, faith and trust go hand in hand. I had to rely on my faith in God to keep my son alive and to accept God's will.

I have a history with God. I can look back over my life and recall times when God has provided for me and has even saved me from myself and my poor decisions. But this issue with Nicholas involved me trusting the intelligence and handiwork of the doctors, while believing in the healing of my Lord. I had to trust my sweet baby with men and women I had never seen before in my life.

I've also learned as a parent, to tailor my expectations per child. Yes, I expect Nicholas to do some core objectives just as his sisters, but my teaching methods had to change for him. I knew things would be different with Nicholas—I just didn't know how much. And never did I consider how often or how much I would have to trust strangers to allow God to work through them on behalf of my baby.

This journey with Nicholas had taught me that my

faith walk has to match my faith talk. It was very important to me that I privately and publically displayed my trust in God. I remember anointing the doorpost of Nicholas' NICU room with oil, believing that God would touch everyone who walked through that door no matter what their personal beliefs.

It's hard enough as a parent to adjust to things not being the way you thought they would be. I didn't have friends coming to the hospital to hold my baby and tell me how much he looks like me. But what I did have were church buddies that would call my cell phone and have me put it in Nicholas' bed as they prayed and petitioned the Lord's healing over him.

I had women from my Victorious Disciples class who would give me money for food and parking at the hospital. Two of my closest friends, who are also the godparents of my children, came and facilitated the most beautiful Baby Dedication Ceremony I have ever seen. My friends and family joined together and hosted A Time of Prayer in my home two days before Nicholas' first open heart surgery.

These are memories that I will treasure forever. Even with my emotions running ragged, I must admit that God is faithful. He has never let me down. I can remember the week that I found out ALL of Nic's hospital doctors were Christians.

While sitting holding Nicholas in the NICU one of the nurses struck up a conversation regarding how much I prayed in her presence. I told her that prayer was the only thing I could offer on my baby's behalf at this time. She then shared with me that Nic's gastro surgeon makes everybody in the operating room stop for prayer before he begins any operation. She went on to say that this doctor didn't care what his coworker's beliefs were; they had to recognize his personal prayer before he operated. I must say I was pleasantly surprised.

Another instance I can recall is with one of the residents on duty when Nicholas was first born. This particular doctor was very matter of fact and quite rigid—never even smiled that I remember. But one Sunday evening while sitting with Nicholas she came by to check on her patients, and she was dressed in a skirt and heels! At first, I didn't even recognize who she was. She would later explain that she stopped by immediately following church.

My ultimate sigh of relief happened late one evening on the very first day that I was able to hold Nicholas. His roommate was also a heart patient. The heart surgeon (who would also be Nic's heart surgeon) had stopped in to check on the baby boy and speak with his parents. The doctor saw me sitting quietly and holding on to my son, so he walked over to ask me to leave so he could speak privately with them. But before I could move, the mother said "please let her stay, because this is the first time she's held her baby."

> I immediately closed my eyes and silently began thanking God for letting me know that trusting Him was not in vain.

And the doctor obliged. While speaking with them I overheard a long list of problems with the little boy's heart—with the bottom line being that his heart was facing in the wrong direction. The mother asked, "Are you going to turn it around?"

And the surgeons response was, "No, I'm not changing the direction of his heart. I'm just going to help it function in the direction God has placed it in."

I immediately closed my eyes and silently began thanking God for letting me know that trusting Him was not in vain. I immediately learned that God loves Nicholas more than I do and He had already stopped by that hospital and hand-selected the team that He would work through in order for my son's conditions to be handled. I realized that I was in a place where there were a lot of prayer warriors and parents who were anticipating, praying, hoping, and trusting---just like me.

I can't go without mentioning that there is also fear, even when you trust God. It was tough to trust every nurse, doctor, and therapist who crossed paths with my baby. I remember coming home one day to shower and finally spend the night in my bed. My mom decided that she would go spend the night with Nicholas and let me spend an evening with the girls.

While calling to check on him before I went to sleep, she advised me that his IV had blown…again. This time all his veins in his hands, arms, and feet had been exhausted. Because hospital policy said that the family has to leave while they insert an IV, my mom didn't have any immediate answers for me as to what the next step was going to be. I remember staying calm and waiting for her to call me back with the outcome.

When she called back, she told me that they had to put the IV in his scalp. Initially I thought that was cruel and unusual. But once again, God already had someone in my life who was a medic that had explained that the scalp was really a better place for it.

I was fine with accepting it—over the phone. However, the following morning when I returned to the hospital and saw my sons head bandaged up like he'd been through a brain surgery, was a different story. I lost it. Completely. I sobbed heavily and was afraid to even hold my sweet boy. Until, in walked my favorite nurse—the same nurse that was Nic's birthing attendant. She had written a poem for me with Nicholas' footprints inside of a heart. It said:

"Dear Mommy,
I know you don't like to see my IV in my head,
So look at my very cute feet instead!!
I promise you Mommy it's better this way;
I can kick and snuggle and move every which way.
Really…It's O.K."

It touched me that she had learned enough about me that she knew I was going to need some encouragement. I was so grateful that God let me know that He trusted Nicholas in their care.

Fear is defined as an unpleasant emotion caused by the belief that someone or something is dangerous, likely to cause pain, or a threat. I had to learn not to allow fear to control me.

Sometimes good-willed people will tell you some

bleak stories about people they know who have been through "the same thing you're going through."

> It's not that I don't have fears—I just try to effectively deal with them.

When they finally finish talking—they think they have helped you. But you're left feeling afraid. I've had people to tell me they have worked with children with special needs and they come across like they have all the answers to my specific situation.

I would like to share with you a few things I have learned that help me handle my fears. Notice that I said "handle." It's not that I don't have fears—I just try to effectively deal with them.

- **Time and Experience**

Professionals can give you statistics regarding treatments and therapies, but living in a situation makes a great difference. I am with my son nearly every day. I have learned how he reacts to various circumstances and situations. I've learned that he handles requests and directives a lot better when he sees his sisters doing the same thing. As his parent, I've noticed that he learns by imitating. So I choose to have him participate with them when picking up toys, climbing stairs, saying his ABC's, dressing himself, etc. Experience has taught me to set him up for success.

- **Don't be Oversensitive**

Sometimes we have to give others the benefit of the doubt. If your child suffers from a condition that makes him look or behave differently, be ready for the looks and stares. Most people can't help themselves from looking and they simply just don't know any better. Purposely embrace others with special needs and disabled children because you share an unexplainable bond.

- **Have Some Expectations**

Of course I have greater expectations for my typical children. But I also have expectations for Nicholas. I expect him to follow directions and to be on task. I realize it may take him longer to grasp a clear understanding and I consider his differences, but he still has appropriate goals that he must meet.

- **Do Not Isolate Yourself Because It's Easier**

Don't be ashamed of what your child cannot do. Embrace what he/she can do. Isolation can cause loneliness, unhappiness, and depression. Physical disabilities offer an added stress, but don't be ashamed to be identified as the parent with a child with disabilities. Instead, research your area for support groups and recreation activities equipped for your child's specific differences.

In an ever changing world it is important that as Christians, we hold on to the Biblical truths and morals we've been taught as we raise our children. I will be the first to admit that without a strong faith in God, I could not parent any of my children. It is unfortunate that often times home, school, and church do not work together.

As a Christian parent it is important that we make all entities work to the advantage of our children. We must lead by example. Children are simply little imitators. As parents we must teach them the ways of the Lord as well as the laws of the land. We must set good examples for them so that God is pleased with our efforts.

In these few years I've been blessed with my own children, I see their ever changing personalities and I count it a blessing that God has trusted me with the assignment to raise them. I'm amazed with how God has created them differently and has put incredible detail into each one.

Now, I won't go without saying that those "details" can tend to be overwhelming at times. Sometimes it even calls for some good old fashioned discipline, readjustments, and consequences.

"Direct your children onto the right path, and when they are older, they will not leave it."
Proverbs 22:6 (NLT)

Each child is different and God requires us to discern what our child needs to learn while on their journey. We must raise our children on purpose, intentionally focusing on their individuality, their emotional needs, and their spiritual needs. By focusing on these areas we build bonds with our children and have open lines of communication. When we do this we set them up for success in school, in relationships with others, and in their spiritual lives.

> For a child with special needs our parenting skills really have to be focused on what is best for their personal success. We have to be their advocate and voice in so many situations.

For a child with special needs our parenting skills really have to be focused on what is best for their personal success. We have to be their advocate and voice in so many situations. I want to share some steps I've taken as a parent that seem to be working so far:

- **Pray**

Pray that God will give you the necessary insight when it comes to every aspect of your child's well being. Pray concerning which doctors to use, therapies to try, foods to give, and functions to attend. This list goes on and on. Pray about everything…God has a way of telling, showing, and leading you in the right direction. It seems like He makes His presence clearly known the more you choose to seek Him.

- **Build a Great Relationship with Your Child**

Take the time to find out what's going on in their life. Consider their thoughts, their friends, and the relationships they build with others. Recognize behavior changes. Have an open line of communication with them. Even if they are non verbal, create your own way of communication, so you will understand any issues and be able to handle them all in a positive way. Remember that children will mimic you—so do the right thing!

- **Build Your Village (support-system)**

It is imperative that you have some help. Parents cannot do or think of everything! It is amazing that God will connect you with the right people at the right time. I have gotten many helpful suggestions from other parents whose children share the same diagnosis, or their family faces the same dynamics as mine. It's easy to connect within the community of special needs and there are always helpful ideas and strategies.

- **Listen To Your Gut**

My mom says, "Follow your first mind." Remember, you know your child better than anyone. If something doesn't feel right—investigate it. Don't be afraid of trying your own remedies, concoctions, and ideas (keeping safety first of course). Sometimes professionals can guide you successfully, but sometimes you have to figure things out through trial and error.

Being a successful Christian parent doesn't mean that you will not feel pressured, defeated, and unsuccessful. Unfortunately, we are often driven by the expectations society has handed us. We often compare ourselves to others without even realizing it.

I encourage you to set your own standards for success based on what is needed for your individual families. I do like to prioritize and set standards and I don't always succeed at the first attempt. I make mistakes like everyone else, but having some goals clearly set gives me a better focus on the direction I'm headed. Having a child that requires "extra attention" means I have to do more planning. But staying consistent as possible seems to be paying off.

> ...when you have a child with special/additional needs, it's not easy or fair to thrust people into your position – especially when you know they really don't have a clue as to what you're faced with from day to day.

Over these past few years, people toss around the phrase "let me know if I can help." Sometimes I think it's just a feel good statement mostly for the person who said it, just so they can be able to say that they offered.

However, there are those within your village who are sincere. I have taken a few friends up on their offers. But when you have a child with special/additional needs, it's not easy or fair to thrust people into your position – especially when you know they really don't have a clue as to what you're faced with from day to day. I'm going to attempt to give some hints and talking points that would be helpful to "special" families like mine:

- **Offer to babysit.** It's hard for me to ask someone outside of family to babysit. Most people immediately think that babysitting means the parent needs to leave their child in your care for an extended about of time—but that's not always the case. I would love to be able to just run a quick errand and leave my kids home with someone I trust. Or be able to have another adult with them while I take a bath, or go for a walk in the neighborhood. Or to actually be able to keep my own doctors appointments.

- **Accept the special needs child the way he/she is.** Sure my son is not going to always behave like other children his age. He just might require more help than his peers. But don't try to change him or my family dynamics in the short time you're around. That will only cause stress on our friendship.

- **Ask before sharing your advice.** Parents are bombarded with advice from professionals, teachers, therapists, etc. And often times we are left feeling like we aren't doing the best that we can for our children. Sometimes unsolicited advice from friends can unknowingly say, "You could be doing a better job."

- **Don't exclude us from activities because we have a child with special needs in our family.** Trust me—I know what settings are appropriate for my child. Believe me –my desire for not being humiliated is much greater than your desire for my child not to embarrass you. At least invite us, and give me the option to gracefully decline.

- **Offer to take care of the siblings.** Having a child in the hospital is tough. But having to juggle the hospital stay and worry about the regular activities at home at the same time makes it even worse. If you know my child is in the hospital, offer to bring a meal or babysit the others, because if I have to ask for help I feel like I'm imposing.

- **Send an encouraging note, text, or email.** It's just good to know that someone is thinking about me. Sometimes I have restless nights and it's good to get a little boost of encouragement along the way.

As a parent of a child with special needs, I have bigger challenges to overcome than I could have ever imagined. And sometimes I feel alone. It's tough trying to balance the needs of everyone else, all at the same time. Coping with circumstances and responsibilities can be overwhelming.

> I truly am grateful for my family, extended family, and friends who step up and help without me even having to ask.

I truly am grateful for my family, extended family, and friends who step up and help without me even having to ask. They have helped me keep my sanity and I really haven't had to miss out on too many events that I've actually wanted to attend.

The last thing that I want to share is a few things I've learned on our first "Summer Break." First of all—there is no break. I used to look forward to being off schedule for a couple months. I'm real good at being lazy.

But this summer I realized that I miss the routine and Nicholas, who thrives off of repetition, just couldn't understand why things drastically and immediately changed. When we don't have a steady flow of "this is supposed to happen next"—things tend to get out of control. During the school year we do very well with our daily routine, however, the summer left me feeling like a bad parent. Let me share what I experienced:

- **Unpredictable Days.** School days come with an expected routine. Summertime however comes with some let's just wing it days because of the relaxed schedule. It was tough for Nicholas to adjust to water parks full of screaming kids, sand between his toes, and sitting in the house watching TV because it was too hot to go outside. His sisters loved these options but poor Nicholas was stir crazy.

- **No Structure.** As much as I would like to believe that I am organized, I obviously don't have the same organizational skills as the teachers and therapists that my son is used to. They didn't have any "do nothing" days, and having a child that is accustomed to structured activities—things can get tough without that structure.

- **New Activities.** Summer programs and activities bring about new teachers, new leaders, new friends, and new expectations. Change is not easily embraced by any child—so for Nicholas it was very difficult. Activities that my daughters considered fun (like an Amusement park) were downright frightening for Nicholas. Being around a new crowd brings about new stares, pointing, and questions.

- **Regression.** With relaxed expectations, regression comes in. I have to remember to offer opportunities for Nicholas to repeat the things he has learned. Just because I think he needs a break, it doesn't mean a break is what's best for him.

- **Lack of Resources.** There are no trained professionals living in my home. Find resources and groups for your child before the summer break begins so that you can make an easy transition.

We didn't get much accomplished during our first official summer break from school. But nobody was injured and we only ended up with one hospital stay, so overall that was pretty good.

No parent wants to make mistakes. We all want our children to be happy, healthy, and well-behaved. I did learn that I have to stay positive and remember that

I am not the only person going through a tough time.

I try to stay connected to other parents through social media and support groups. There is always somebody who is going through something similar to me and my family.

> **Having a desired parenting theory is fine as long as you remember children have their own personalities and they need time to express themselves. Most often, their plan doesn't line up with yours.**

I've learned that expectations are just expectations. If thing's don't go as expected, so be it, and try again tomorrow. As parents we also have to be flexible and don't resist change. Don't be the parent who wants everything to be perfect and in order, because you will go crazy!

Having a desired parenting theory is fine as long as you remember children have their own personalities and they need time to express themselves. Most often, their plan doesn't line up with yours. Kids change from day to day. Just remember that being flexible, doesn't mean to be inconsistent. You just may discover a different way of doing things that ends up being a win-win situation for all.

> *"But Jesus overheard them and said to Jarius, "Don?t be afraid. Just have faith."*
>
> Mark 5:36 (NLT)

One thing that we can be sure of is that all babies grow, develop, make changes, and learn. Even if your child does these things at a slower rate just try to provide more opportunities for learning and developing to take place.

It has helped me to incorporate home, church, and school in teaching Nicholas and myself and my family to deal with his diagnosis. Research continues to show that early intervention services are extremely helpful. Families can benefit from information, support groups, and government services.

Remember that the Individuals with Disabilities Education Act requires all states to develop programs to service your child. Be mindful that the program should include children with and without disabilities. This is commonly called mainstreaming. This helps the child with the disability to gain social confidence, and acceptance, and the child without a disability to look past the differences and learn to respect all people.

I remember a social worker encouraging me to put

Nicholas in a public setting such as soccer or basketball within our neighborhood. She said, "When he gets to school, he will be known as Nic...not as the kid with a disability."

As she pointed out—let people get to know him for who he is, not for his diagnosis. Also, try your best to be patient and to seek wisdom. Practicing patience develops our heart muscles. Don't expect to make the right decision the first time, or every time. But as you learn your child, this process will become easier and more comfortable.

As a family, do your best to stick together. Everyone in the family plays an important role. I am referring to the family in the home and the family outside of the home (the village). Nicholas has a personality that people fall in love with. So he has family at home, at church, at school, even at the barbershop. And we are all on one accord when it comes to Nicholas—he will learn. And we are committed to teaching him.

I hope that one day Nicholas will understand how blessed he is to have two sisters. One is two years older than him; the other is two minutes older than him. And they both love their brother unconditionally. They treat him as an equal part of our family, and that's exactly how he wants to be treated. We've learned to fill in the gaps for each other and to make sure that Nicholas isn't left out.

Finally, I encourage you to change other people's expectations. It is unfortunate that society has some preconceived ideas of what a person with disabilities should look and act like.

I have chosen to help Nicholas fool the world. When he was first born and doctors, nurses, and social workers were giving me the run down of what to expect, I knew they meant well, but they were giving me clinical answers. I didn't think anyone knew how I truly felt, or that they really understood my parental concerns.

> I remember whispering in Nicholas' ear that if he would "fight hard, I would pray hard, and he would fool the world." At that time I could have never imagined how much Nicholas would teach me about the world we live in, about the dynamics of a family, or about relationships with others.

I remember whispering in Nicholas' ear that if he would "fight hard, I would pray hard, and he would fool the world." At that time I could have never imagined how much Nicholas would teach me about the world we live in, about the dynamics of a family, or about relationships with others.

It causes you to trust a Power much greater than yourself. Enjoy your journey. Embrace your child. And forever trust God.

Steal Away to Some Secret Place

When my heart is heavy and my burdens hard to bear,
And there's no earthly being with whom my load to share,
I steal away to some secret place and have a talk with God,
For He is the One who knows the path
these weary feet have trod.

While in this secret chamber on bended knees, I pray,
"Lord, keep me in the path of righteousness
on this and every day.
Deliver me from all evil and let thy will be done.
Grant me a home in thy kingdom when this race is run."

As I quietly and tearfully kneel there, He gently lifts my load
And gives me strength and courage to keep on down the road,
Toward that Celestial City with its beautiful pearly gates,
Where my Savior and my loved ones for me await.

So when your burdens are heavy
and storm clouds darken your way,
When friends have turned their backs
and all manner of evil they say,
Just when you think all hope is gone
and your load you cannot bear,
Steal away to some secret place and pray...
God is always there.

Fredna Hadley Allen
(Anita Allen-Penn's grandmother)

About Dr. Anita Allen-Penn

"For I know the plans I have for you," declares the Lord, "plans to prosper you and not to harm you, plans to give you hope and a future."
Jeremiah 29:11

Dr. Anita A. Penn has spent years motivating and inspiring individuals of all ages and walks of life to get out of their comfort zone and get a front row seat in life through our Lord and Savior Jesus Christ balanced with maximizing all potentials.

While working several dead-end jobs, with the support of her family she moved to Texas where she returned to college and completed her undergraduate degree. Following college she returned back to Flint, MI where she was raised and educated and ironically taught in the same classroom her mother taught in. After a few years, with a desire to move back to the Dallas area she gained employment with American Airlines where she served for 10 years.

In 2009, she maximized the opportunity and need to

become a stay at home mom to her three children Nadia, Nia, and Nicholas. With the demanding special medical needs that came along with her son Nicholas is what ultimately caused her bold confession to "trust, lean, and maximize her relationship with her Savior"—and the calling to ministry was birthed within her.

Dr. Anita is a graduate of Jarvis Christian College of Hawkins, TX and earned her PhD in Urban Ministries from Aspen Theological College and Seminary; Aspen, CO.

Currently she attends the Greater Mt. Pleasant Baptist Church under the leadership of Dr. David Henderson, Jr., where she serves as the Director of Ministries. She enjoys volunteering with Amazing Little Hearts parent support group of Medical City Children's Hospital and the National Down Syndrome Society of Tarrant County. She also enjoys tutoring children that are functioning below reading level.

With special thanks

To my Mom, Janis Collins Allen, for your prayers, late night talks, early morning tears, unending support, and forever encouraging words of wisdom.

To my children, Nadia, Nia, and Nicholas, for the life-changing lessons you teach me daily and for loving me.

To Jeffery Holmes, for your hard work as my "unofficial assistant" and my voice of reason.

To Jalmera Barber, for attending every doctor appointment and educational team meeting—a little boy couldn't ask for a better "T.T."

To my prayer partner and battle buddy, Adrienne Leary, for keeping me lifted in prayer no matter what.

To Pastor David Henderson, Elmerine Allen Bell, William Allen, Jr., Ramona Bishop-Burton, Autry Johnson, and the entire Village of People who love me and my children and who stand in the gap for us through encouragement and prayer.

In loving memory of my grandmothers, Carrie Loeb Collins, Fredna Hadley Allen, and E. Elaine Burks, who taught me how to love unconditionally.

Searchlight Press
Who are you looking for?
Publishers of thoughtful Christian books since 1994.
PO Box 554
Henderson, TX 75652-0554
214.662.5494
www.Searchlight-Press.com
www.JohnCunyus.com

Discipling Through Your Disability, 113

www.ingramcontent.com/pod-product-compliance
Lightning Source LLC
Chambersburg PA
CBHW070531100426
42743CB00010B/2044